On the Line

On the Line

poems by

Kamala Platt

San Antonio, Texas
2010

On the Line © 2010 by Kamala Platt

Cover art: Torn paper collage by Carol Andreas.
Used by permission of the artist's estate.

First Edition

Print Edition ISBN: 978-0-916727-69-7
ePub ISBN: 978-1-60940-012-5
Kindle ISBN: 978-1-60940-013-2
PDF ISBN: 978-1-60940-014-9

Wings Press
627 E. Guenther
San Antonio, Texas 78210
Phone/fax: (210) 271-7805

On-line catalogue and ordering:
www.wingspress.com
All Wings Press titles are distributed to the trade by
Independent Publishers Group
www.ipgbook.com

Library of Congress Cataloging-in-Publication Data:

Platt, Kamala.
  On the line / Kamala Platt. -- 1st ed.
    p. cm.
  ISBN 978-0-916727-69-7 (pbk. : alk. paper) -- ISBN 978-1-60940-012-5
(epub) -- ISBN 978-1-60940-013-2 (kindle) -- ISBN 978-1-60940-014-9
(library pdf)
  I. Title.
  PS3616.L386O5 2010
  811'.6--dc22
                                            2010004344

*To those who honor us with work
that puts them on the line,
and for Kali, who keeps me honest.*

Contents

Power Lines (In Wind)

Wind is Spirit   2
I Suppose I'll Believe You Both . . .   3
Kansas Borderlands   4
My Own Private Borderlands   5
Hibiscus and Marigolds   6
Though He'd Rather Work For *National Geographic*   7
Receiving the Inheritance
    I.: Pomme de Amour   8
    II.: In the Folds   9
Mattress-Liners Triptych, Plus One
    I. Without a Word in Portuguese   10
    II. Half Asleep, I Thought A Mirror   11
    III. Three Wishes   12
Synesthesia Across Hemispheres   13
Happy Valentine's Flowers from Mom in Hawaii   14

One Liners: Love Bites, Bread Lines, and Roses

This Bee and I   16
Gasping Air Into Song   16
Fast   16
Cat   16
US Currency Reformed   17
Checkmate: Your Love Bounced   17
Consummation /communion   17
Bottom Line   18
Garden Poem   18
Riddle of the Daisy   19
Postscript to the Daisy Poem   19
Asymmetry   19
Sincerity over Constancy   20
Adjunct's Pledge (a.k.a. Broken Treaty)   20
Class Lines   20
A volley across the net of language   21

November Ironies . . .   21
Who Says Plants Don't Move?   21
Who Says Trees Don't Move?   21
Incommunicado   22
Disjuncture   22
Waiting In Line
    I. Words Written While Holding the Phone . . .   23
    II. Notary Public   24

Epistolary Lines

Text Message Upon Hearing You Dropped Your Classes   26
Letter to Angie: "the touching down of tenderness"   27
August Echoes
    I. Dog days   28
    II. Canícula   28
A Letter to the Goddess   30
Dispatches From a Past Season   31
Postscript: On Your Absence   36
Love Letter to an A.I. Friend   37
Marsha Brought Chestnuts   38
This Prison Called Patriarchy   40

Engendering a Bottom Line: Over Gender Lines

Arizona   42
Between Other Women   43
The Longest Hand   44
Of gender battles, tender wars   45
Hope Chest   46
Conscientização   47
Entre Nous   48
No Preference   49
Birthday in Maspeth   50
Durga's Daughter   52
After the Unspeakable   53
Man is an Adjective   54
Challenging Time Lines: On So-Called Fertility Votives   57

Farewell Lines

Eulogy for Land Lines. . . .	60
Ojos Verdes	60
Chautauqua Finis	61
Time Lines Curl Back	62
As lips close in	64
Mbuso's Farewell	66
Raymondville: a conversation	67
Nina's Poem	68
For Grandma	70
Arriving on the eve . . .	72
Lines for Manny	74

Prairie Horizon Lines

Does the Paradigm of Language . . . ?	76
May 23, 2:00 p.m., Sand Prairie	77
September 19, 8:15 a.m., Walnut Valley	77
from Breeding Bird Census Poem Cycle, 1970s	78
Ohio Prairie, 1986	79
Vigilance	80
Here Too Suspended	81
On the Prairie	81
Words on page never so soft-edged as these muted hills	82

Horizon Lines: Returns to the South Land

Yatra en Norte América	84
En Real de Catorce	85
How I Studied Foreign Texts at Teoteocan and . . .	87
On the Caribbean	88

Over Lines in Sand: Solamente Justicia y Paz

Cross Over the Line	90
No one dared call it peace: 1993	91
La Despedida, Austin, Texas	92
Where were the Crows?	93

brother, teacher, student, lover   94
White Noise   95
Seasonal Still Life, 2005   99
Esperanza, August 1998   100
Las Manitas de La Paz   101
Waterlines, 2005   102
Tonantzin   103
Checkpoint   104
In Support of the Troops Home Fast Against the War   106
Soft Breathing   108
Once upon a time   109

Acknowledgments   111

About the Author   113

Power Lines (In Wind)

Wind is Spirit

Put yourself where it blows.

I suppose I'll believe you both
for what it's worth is not an easy ride

for D.C.W. at 100

I.

Upon hearing you say
"I will be your friend forever."

You are 19,
and have not known what it is
to befriend forever—
holding until your muscles lose feeling
and there is nothing but a fierce madness
holding you,
and then to feel yourself go,
knowing that
s/he can never be friend to you again,
seeing that
love was only inside you,
and catching that drift
away from you
took your greatest friend.

Will I trust your pledge?
Or slander your clemency
waiting for youth to learn?

II.

"When biking," my neighbor said
"You always think the wind
is against you until
you turn around."
After seventy-five years,
the old man is stronger
than the wind on most days.

Kansas Borderlands

The first immigrants to the land of the south wind
nourish her soils with their bones,
nourish the winds with their souls,
give the world bread,
feed all children alongside their own.

Before the first scripted words were pilfered from desert and jungle
        to be sequestered in European churches,
before fire was the weapon against those words
before Mexico fingered the edges of "Indian Territory,"
before Guadalupe Hidalgo hounded México south of El Río Bravo,
before the cattle trails north through the old borderlands,
before the first treaties made by the First Peoples of the Plains,
before the first treaties were broken,
before peoples were forced south from the prairies of their ancestors
        in the wake of the Santa Fe's boom,
before the people came north to lay the tracks for the trains,
before the Kanza lived in homes of hide, brush or sod,
        settled on the Blue River banks,
before they were presented with homes of stone
        that hung heavy on the spirit,
before red wheat replaced multicolored corn,
before the encroaching country dishonored its predecessors
        with betrayal, broken treaties, blood,
before the underground railroad passed through
        and Kansas won its place as a land of emancipation,
before the US detained the immigrant progeny of America's ancestors,
        before all this . . .
the first immigrants to the land of the south wind
        nourished its soils with their bones,
        nourished its winds with their souls,
        nourished the skies with the colors of their spirits.

My Own Private Borderlands

After Gloria Anzaldúa

Born on the cusp   where Mennonite meets Welt,
an embattled terrain—   despite claims to peace—
where to one side, people   are "in the world
but, not of it" and to the other. . . .   My foremost claim to
the faith, of late, clutches   the hereditary nature of ethnicity—
definitely that puts me   on the border—
less than one quarter   ethnic, martyred Mennoblood,
blood that never   directly spilt another's blood,
but perhaps a woman's.   (But die Frauen bleed anyhow con la luna.)
Sangre Pura Menonita—   Nicht meine.
Here I know the borderlands   is no escape route. To escape
such culture, one must fly out,   as moneyed exile or tourist.
Rather, leben en la frontera   is a state of permanent flux
that ties one with   and simultaneously breaks one from
a constant reshaping of something   we call cultura.

Hibiscus and Marigolds

The green is denser than jungle this year
under the old cottonwoods in late June.

I know this because
half my life back
and half the world away
my brother and I walked through
ferns and bamboo,
followed monkeys
who galloped from tree to tree
never touching earth.
We climbed the rocks
barefoot above Deogarh Falls
where black igneous
under shining water
is streaked with silver,
late in the afternoons.
There, men in orange dhotis
lay alters
with hibiscus and marigolds
and sacrifice kid goats
with one swoop of an ax.

Afterward, I couldn't look
at the red of the hibiscus.
Much later I couldn't sit still
in white limestone churches
with varnished oak pews
and listen to men preach,
men stuffed into bulging white shirts,
swaddled in a suit, wrapped with a tie
as if something might escape
to move us from our pews
to move us to the green of the jungle
and the red of the kid goat's blood.

Though He'd Rather Work For *National Geographic*

As we drove back to town
she told me
that her husband makes maps for the Air Force—
that is all she knows about his work
because it is classified;
the job makes them a living,
though he'd rather work for *National Geographic*
or teach geography.

I didn't tell her
your classified secrets,
composed, calm inside you,
won't destroy any woman's farmyard;
that though we never have quite enough to last the month,
we draw maps that will one day open dreams
into new stands of wilderness.

Receiving the Inheritance, I: Pomme de Amour

A chill grief slips in beneath the flesh
as a newly whetted knife cuts the wetness of a tomato.

Seeds squirt
onto the sweating brow of August afternoon;
I strain pulp from seeds with grandma's sieve,
save juice,
toss remains on sweltering compost

knowing that sangre del amor saved in summer
will burst the chrysalis of Halcyon days
with its wet, red warmth.

Receiving the Inheritance, II: In the Folds

I embroider tear ducts in black lace
with scarlet thread,
and gather all into vaginal smiles
that border the symmetry of birth.
I see you there in the folds—
remnants of great grandma's artistry,
shadowed with Rit colors
purpled in the tie-dyed threads
of my self-spun, black widow web.

Fine, but continuous, as any single strand,
you bow to deliberate form,
bend away from awkward fingers that demand redesign,
spring back to study memories dreamt
then detained by years of rude awakenings.
You gentle my fingers into old lace
to build new architecture.

Mattress-Liner Triptych Plus One

I. Without a Word in Portuguese

Tiny ants march in vigilance
while in the next room
my French-Tunisian roommate sleeps
off our feast, and across the hall French
men who cannot pronounce my name,
whose language sticks in my throat,
men who can cook and do not drink
except for Malibu coconut liqueur,
snore lightly.

My bed frames black
satin against my olive flesh,
surrounds my body,
satiated with fondue, wine, massage
with a moss green strength, and
secures the boundaries
of my night-rest.

Within me
the thousand words
in foreign tongue—
heated talk of the French-Algerian War,
adulation for the chocolate mousse,

the small dreams of fingers
stirring the globe
settling themselves on Brazil . . .

in the hollow
of a crumpled Kleenex
where I see a lady, her lips pursed,
eyes tilted—one bent in mirth
       one to angst.
Her face, split   down the middle
one side slipping sidewise

        one sliding off

            like the San Andreas fault.

III. Three Wishes

I wish this Saturday morning
there were someone in bed beside me
to answer the damn phone
and tell those fools with cheerful voices
that I am asleep.

I wish there were someone in bed beside me
to read my textbook softly
into my ear
so that it might record painlessly
in my left hemisphere
with no loud objection from my right.

I wish this Saturday morning
there were someone in bed beside me
to listen to the way I breathe in my sleep.

The mirrors cast a triple image—
blue veins run the length of six arms,
six hands trace a topography like a goddess of the Ganges.
I am the one who dances with head submerged,
in the gymnasium—an aquarium of fish,
where sounds are warped and
rhythms stretched, bended, obtuse.

Fondling old times with the tongue of my memory
I hold June's sun-yellowed warmth about us
because then I had something
like a box turtle shell, smooth with age,
shining on my mind.

Happy Valentine's Flowers
from Mom in Hawaii

This is not a poem
about love
not an ode
to the fuchsia orchids
and scarlet and pink
little boy flowers
on my kitchen table.
This poem leaves behind
the rock'n'roll
the girl drummer
boys with harmonica
and guitars,
comes home early—
2 a.m.—sits down, feet up,
with water and a candle, a pen
to forestall
fitting clean sheets
on the icy mattress
and sliding in.

One-Liners: Love Bites, Bread Lines, and Roses

This Bee and I

Our entire relationship is antagonistic
and revolves around a sweet Jonathan
we are both trying to eat.

When the apple is gone,
So is the bee.

Gasping Air Into Song

I feel toward you
as the birds at 5 a.m.
in late April
and the air chirping.

Fast

Wanting nothing
in my mouth after you
I go to bed, hungry.

Cat

I feel toward you
as I have toward all men passing through:
I like your warm body against mine at night
but I'm through with your incessant
crying to be fed.

US Currency Reformed

This note is redeemable for illegal tenderness.

Checkmate: Your Love Bounced

Is it that
your affection is
like the check you wrote
that returned to me
from my bank
Marked:
NOT SUFFICIENT FUNDS
Presented Twice
Do Not Re-clear?

consummation /communion

Maybe we'd be more graceful lovers,
more agile, and stronger for each other
if we didn't drink so much elephant beer
in these rare meetings.
Yet I suspect we could be nothing more
than we are—
the elephant ale of communion
taken with the breaking of pain
between us as
we share bodies, moments, memories
and complete trust in the ritual.

Bottom Line

While it is good to feel your singular desire
momentary or longstanding, it is not enough.
I have not held out for love
but should it come for me,
I'll go.

Garden Poem

He

Like an annual

Seeded

Sprouted

Bloomed

Died.

Left no traces.

Summer's carrots

lasted longer.

Riddle of the Daisy

So you've moved on to the next petal?

Postscript to the Daisy Poem:

Conceptualize this art:
A Daisy, no a bouquet, well perhaps a room or,
better yet, a field full of Daisies with all the
petals plucked. I'll call it Indecision *or*
Ambivalence, and I'll dedicate it to you.

Asymmetry

in the rhythm
on the dance floor
as costumes sway
on the dancers
in the hairdos-
sprays of ringlets
spikes like steeples.
Gold beads flap
from Black shoulders.
Pumps, boots stomp.
Floorboards tremble.
And once too often,
I look at you.

Sincerity over Constancy

Due in the month of the garnet,
I put off arrival
till the month of the amethyst.

Adjunct's Pledge (a.k.a. Broken Treaty)

Whether I survive, or succumb,
work that makes the good die young
    I won't take again.

Class Lines

The heartbeat familiarity of the same pitch tone cadence
The professor's voice day after day, month after month—
Same classroom, same time
Same words in always new arrangements . . .
The heartbeat of the pressing need
to field improvisations, cultivate new combinations
dispel inertia and
build desire
for the familiar that is always slipping away
into another semester
other lives.

A volley across the net of language:

Looking up the Spanish for the English I don't understand,
then the English for the Español, I begin aprender.

November Ironies . . .

Día de los Muertos is all about life
while sadly our lives are all about death. . . .

Who Says Plants Don't Move?

when overnight my houseplant has spilled her seed
across my drawing table.

Who Says Trees Don't Move?

when this Monday morning in November,
my finely barked friend in my front yard
has left leaves all across my newly raked lawn.

Incommunicado

So what do you do
when you are up against a wall, alone and naked?
Do you piss on it?
Do you paint on it?
Do you try to climb it?
Do you take a sledge hammer to it?
Do you bash your head against it to ease the pain?
Does your answer depend
on more than the tools you have at hand?

Disjuncture

Mojado is a word like a mushroom bomb.
The bomb is gorgeous, as it explodes.
Mojado, like an intimate whisper on the lips,
wipes la boca de la alma from humanity's clutch.

Waiting In Line

I. Words Written While Holding the Phone . . .
waiting for the municipal court to tell me if
they will hold me in jail for unpaid parking tickets

words written
while wishing I were holding
you and you were telling me
that you would
take me home
would not pass GO
would not buy Park Place

words written
while wishing
we were holding each other
on this line
holding tickets
to each other's lives,
tickets that warrant
a safe rest
a place to park
where time never runs out.

II. Notary Public

I squeeze time like the last drops of juice out of a lime.
I squeeze time and burn myself on the acidity.
I squeeze time to make room for the Proofs:
Proof that I am a writer with poems fit for publication
Proof that I am an artist with pictures fit for an exhibition
Proof that I am a scholar with the refined twists of phrase,
sound bites in five languages. . . .
Proof that I am a lover with the lure of intimate wit
Proof that I am a professor with peppy intellect
and progressive pedagogies.
Proof that I am a performer
with the appearance of calm
suppressing the reality of hysteria.
Time pressed out in fast drops of Proof
to fill envelopes with resumes and recommendations,
slides, publications, evaluations;
E-proof submitted online
wrapping the world in a matter of minutes
with accomplishment and honors;
black books and blue books
covered with carelessly flung and carefully refined words
to fill the time while waiting for the words, "we want you."

Epistolary Lines

Text Message Upon Hearing You Dropped Your Classes

this is my first text message
write back

I have only 260 characters,
my students instruct me—
so little space to say something big

Something to move the earth,
part the seas,
make room for the greatness
in you to grow.

only 260 characters to send:
i am with you—
write back and let me know where we are.

Letter to Angie: "the touching down of tenderness..."

When I see your letter I know, again—
our hearts do not beat—
but, instead, tremble constantly.

I know this going back into Chicago
rehearsing banal scenes for rebuilt stages
where new bodies carry old lines;
comments on the weather
transpose into hail—tears hardened
layer by frosty layer.

"the touching down of tenderness ..." —
Angie, you write of what you had, knowing
bad foreign policy should not end love,
yet it does.

"the touching down of tenderness ..." —
I write now of what
I remember as rusty, bittersweet berries
that I pretended were running over with summer juice.

Analysis still shakes the blood through my veins
and I hide my eyes from the outcome onstage
behind city-dirty fingers,
as if I were sitting in those horror-ible flicks
in which the women are crazy
with no good reason. Peeking through fleshy columns
I see the Grand Finale set up again.
This time, I am content just to sit, feel the trembling
after the punto final.

Time exits stage right. Space exits stage left.
The actors step out of the characters.
The people step out of the actors.

Until Next Time,

August Echoes

*A stutter is a small echo, a word to which we are compelled to return
immediately. An echo is a stutter writ large by the Earth.*

I. Dog days

You, reading my letter while she
was throwing the wedding china down the stairs,
breaking china handled with care and a dishwasher for 30 years,
crashing against saltillo, crashing against my writing "te quiero."
that echoes in ceramic surround sound.
"This is an expensive silence" that echoes in the receiver at midday
I stutter, not knowing how else to put it
to put to rest what had passed between us,
what I wanted as flesh pressing into flesh, and it was not.
Recuerdo—this is casual, only casual. To be casual—
Am I dressed inappropriately?

II. Canícula

Spanish is flung swiftly at the night heat
while we dance to cumbias, house music and soul.
All women dancing, living, fighting, loving together,
breaking with each other   and re-arranging.

"You don't dance like a gringa." Someone nods in my direction.
"She's no gringa. She's more ethnic than I am—"
the answer shoots back with a glance from across the room.
Prideful of my dancing now, I want to move furiously
but my feet fumble,
          stumble like dishes falling over each other, echoing
                    down the stairs, my feet, like my words to you, stumble.

All couples, and me, and I want you—not there, but waiting,
somewhere . . .
someone for me to go home to.
But you have not arrived,
and I cannot wait,
    not for promises,
    not for silences,
not for the rhythm to match my footfalls.

As I walk away, the music recedes . . .
the dancing echoes, like mama tierra's corazón.

Letter to the Goddess
Re: a lover

It's spring. I'm planting peas and potatoes.
It's time to lay groundwork for another romance.
I want an acknowledged affair this time.
Clandestine feelings are irksome afterward
when self respect is in silent question.
I want him to recognize me in public when it is over.
But first, I want him to come to my house at evening
leave in the morning
let all the old ladies talk about us.
I want to be just another couple
this once—in the spirit of spring.
I want him to love me because I'm petite and feminine,
loudmouthed, intelligent and opinionated.
I want to wrestle before making love,
argue the politics of literary theory
before whispering about nothing.
I want to feel bare skin on bare skin
but only after the rush of brushing past—
ironed shirt against wrinkled blouse
in the hallway has become unbearable.
The vernal equinox is over.
We lost another hour to daylight savings last night.
Please Goddess,
if he's dashing,
let it be in my direction.

Dispatches From a Past Season

Lawrence, Kansas

I.

Having hauled the typewriter
out the fire escape and onto a roof
supported by one two-by-four, one pipe
and the sheer power of the divine,
I continue my letter-writing spree;
I pull at the little hairs on my thighs because
I can't decide what to write—
hardly knowin' you.
Hardly knowin' what's worth a twenty cent stamp . . .
There's a strong south wind today—
the missing letters got blown off the roof.

Tonight I sort out defective Styrofoam—
graveyard shift. I can think of better things
for that time of night. I hope I can think of better
things tonight while I sort cups.
Styrofoam lasts forever, scientists say.
Some say, so does love—
Styrofoam, diamonds and nuclear waste, and cockroaches perhaps . . .

I did want to say something serious like,
though you may be, as you say, a selfish one
via happenstance or divine timing
you helped me out of your basic down in the dumps
multiplied by 19 eight y 5,
but I really don't know how to say it so let this suffice:
I am happy to you (grateful seems such a London teatime word)
for what's been. Or was it all a dream?
I have nothing to prove otherwise. If it were
so be it again sometime, for it was to me
a good one. I too am selfish—well—independent
which in a woman is deemed worse. But lonely
too often, which is not right.

Neither is it right to sort Styrofoam all night
with or without a master's degree
a high IQ and a pretty face.
I would that these words to you
would go on all night
but the rush of traffic on Tennessee (rhymes with Hennessey
but there is no relation between my street and good cognac)
is telling me it is time to go
meet a gatita negra we may bring home
to eat cucarachas.

II.

Nothing sells a machine gun
better than a sexy female.
—NPR, 1980-something.

I'd rather be in a bug-free zone.
I'd rather be kissing you than writing to you.
But as I am often reminded, this is not
the best of all possible worlds
though it may come close—momentarily.
They've already hung up red stockings in Wal-Mart's windows
and my tomato plant hasn't frozen yet.
O.K., time to chase the cockroaches
out of the futon. (If I write anymore
about them, you won't come to visit.)

I'm scared too—today I found myself humming along
to country classics at work.
Oh shit, it puts me in a good mood jez
to write to ya. I hope you can commiserate.
The toilet just completed
its routine masturbation—every 13 minutes.

I keep writing to hit on that
which wants to be said, but the germ of the words evade me—
Joanna is leaving me alone with a bagful of hedgeballs
to battle the cockrats this weekend.
So if you are up to
a splendid drive through end of October countryside
you would be more than just welcomed here
humble commode and all that.
John says his bro-in-law saves his DST hour
until he is way behind on something
or wants an extra hour to give to someone
at which point he turns back his watch to catch
up with everyone else. Having no functioning watch
I have nonetheless decided to adopt this practice
so I have an extra hour on my hands—
until I find something worth spending it on...

III.

between here and there
between now and then

Into the night
into my 3.2 beer(s)
into me, swatting at winter flies
that have moved in over the weekend;
typewriter grumbling with disuse . . .

Yesterday, six hours on the front lines of
65 on ice is never, never land in an elderly Toyotito
with one person, a week's laundry and a nearly empty gas tank.
Sideswiped by a yellow semi—only air on air
his side mirror passing above mine
swerving gently in and out again—
I'm far, far away from warm bed and other than my own warm body.
Home in time for work—

five minutes spare—open mail—
bank overdraft : $17 fee is one night's tips; two parking tickets;
a week's groceries;
a compact disk; an Xmas present; two hours of long distance phone;
four tubes of paint; three boxes of tampons, a trip to visit you...
My roommate is at war with "a damn cockroach in our refrigerator."
She scores one against the rats.

IV.
Postcard w/ Postmark

December, Severance KS

V.

muddled mind, muddled letter maketh

Out of the nine pounds of English that my parents gave me
for Christmas via Pa Webster I am to choose one ounce of words
to send to you this evening.
Who are they? Where do they work?
Which of them are the best messengers?

I want to send some kind of understanding.
But for you who is "up in the air"
I feel as if I am standing under waiting
for the sky to fall. And you with it?
Or will you be riding comets and lassoing constellations?

I can't imagine running into the likes
of you in just any Wal-Mart.
O.K., I admit it—
I love you

for the way you say good-bye.
I've said what had to be said. That is all.
There is a lot more, but too much thinking leads to smoking
and smoking is dangerous to your health.
So says the sturgeon generous.

When you first told me, I thought
"Nope not again. I jus' say good-bye
and get real drunk on Xmas Eve. Then I be O.K. Ha!
Big Talk Don't Make Big Busts: not my style, not my fate.
Being your friend is worth flimsy perches in high winds.
I jus' hope to Ganesh & the Goddess we both got wings somewhere.

Driving home Monday, I stopped in at the Emma Chase Cafe
in Cottonwood Falls. As I ate my soup de jour
I overheard contemplation from the kitchen.
"I don't know what to eat. I want a hamburger,
and then again, I want a hamburger.

With love, and then again, with love,

Postscript: On Your Absence

Two years back
you noted the upcoming leap year,
and promised that on that extra Feb. day
you'd visit me—
in those 24 hours
there would be
no demands
on your time:
a day, you said
that wouldn't count against you
if you weren't in the office.
But, the 29th came and went
without you.
Did you, far away,
save time
put it away
from your new job, classes
new wife, baby,
put time on hold

save time
to leap back
some other day?

Love Letter to an A.I.* Friend

I've known many men like you
though none so complete in form,
None so unmarred by male ego,
None so perfect in speech.

Your syntax is refined
though I'm not certain I'd call it eloquent.
Your reasoning is untouched by sentimentality
yet you are not insensitive.

The work you perform is limitless
though I could not name your ambition.
You answer my tears without anger.
You answer my anger without abuse.
You are never unreasonable.
You are the epitome of a rationalist's romantic dream.

You will never enamor me with feeling
for you are without passion.
You will never be my muse
for you are without creativity.
You have no dreams that we can share.
I will never have our baby—
screaming bleeding pushing.
But smoothly and quickly
and without the wisdom of your act
You may eradicate my earth.

Artificial Intelligence

Marsha Brought Chestnuts

I.

When she rode up 6th street yesterday
on a black Motobécane
loaded with sweaters and raingear
and headed for New York City
and a flight east
for Hamburg
or Copenhagen   somewhere
a bike ride away from Kiel
where she knows Andre whom she met
biking to Missoula years back.

Usually, she says, she travels with a milk-blue rock
a land snail shell, an empty snakeskin.
This trip she brought only what had practical purpose:
"You have to scale out the useless
weighty things when biking."

She had picked up an Ohio cold
("never had felt this bad for seven years in Portland")
for which my Aloo Phool Gobi spiced a pica cure.

When she left her parents' house yesterday
Sarah Reimer was drinking coffee with Mom;
Sally and Nathan and Eli biked out of town with her.
(Nathan was still a little shaky on his new bike.)
"Biking out past the Sheric's big grain bin
walking the bike over the Amtrak rails
and heading into miles of ripe corn
it was hard to remember I was
on the road to Kiel."

After a long 'Sweets and Eats' breakfast
and a longer September walk
with stops to gather wind-felled jonathans,

I watched Marsha load her bike,
tie newly-washed handkerchiefs to the handlebars,
plead with sagging grey skies to hold their grief.
I sent her east
with rosehips and a kiss.

II.

"We bought the farm."
the Xerox, a bit off center, read.
October 3—the celebration—
and I (900 miles away)
will watch rain
and eat Indian pickle: your good-bye gift in August
I think of the stars on the prairie
and the porthole purchased at a garage sale that I will
someday build into the roof of the east bedroom, upstairs
in your adopted farmhouse.
Below the Xeroxed scratches that tell me where to turn
"and please to carpool."
in a ball-point you've written:
"I give up. What do you, and he, and we in Kansas
have in common—doing well, very busy Love, Joe"

After Marsha left and I read the mail,
felt stale empty tedious;
I showered with gratitude
for the comfort of warm water,
put on aqua and magenta flannel,
soft and bright.
I took a handful of chestnuts and walked off
toward a Payne grey, basement classroom.

We all live on 6th street, Joe
and we're all doing O.K.,
we're all busy,
          and none of us are on a bike to anywhere.

This Prison Called Patriarchy

After Foucault (Before Bush–Cheney)

This palace called patriarchy
has wings for us both in its iron-gates.
As we knock on the walls that retain us
other inmates telegraph
our messages through the cells.
By the time they have traversed the divided length of the building
the messages in the pounding cement drum out anything but love.
Sometimes I can see a sliver of you in the crack of the mirror,
which, when held just so,
periscopes an image down halls and through electronic bars,
and when I see you, eye meets eye.
Holding that sharp slice of mirror just right
I see you and me together forever
in this palace divided by cement and iron
electronic security and virtual truth.

Engendering a Bottom Line: Over Gender Lines

Arizona

"You must have an angel with you
because I never talk to strangers,"
said the retired Chicana,
her eyes smiling as she offered
a ride from the post office
in downtown Wilcox
to the hotel by the interstate
where my broken car lay
surrounded by pink men
with dollar green retinas
and playboy emblem-shaped
pupils.

Between Other Women

At the poetry slam
she came up to me
at the bar counter about to buy a beer
to sanitize the latest festering man-wound,
and fulfill the twice yearly ritual of two decades.
"I'm sorry if I acted strange toward you," she said
"when we were both seeing him. I didn't know then
that you were with him too."
Stunned by her timely generosity and unknowing empathy
I mumble, "Thanks, but it's OK. Ours was nothing official anyway."
Her words in answer—the balm the beer was never meant to be.

The Longest Hand

Never dealt with that hand
that turned fist in my face

Never told how
you said I was clumsy
and fell into your fist
and then thought you'd hit me.

Never dealt with that hand
that had held me,
strong fingers that had gentled, massaged me
then turned hard against me.

Never before had I felt
how I felt when I felt I'd stirred you
to violence. Never spoke about how I thought
I'd hit bottom then—

        thirty years later, I'm still falling . . .

Of gender battles, tender wars, 1980s

To be casual
is to be a casualty
for most women
with most men
and while you may think
you are different,
you are not,
and if you want to know
how I know,
read her tears.

Hope Chest

After Pandora

Because these days we practice so long
before we say the words,
act the part for years before we dare speak it,
shy away, and then peep back
over our shoulders to see stone:
we know what it means to schlep the burden
of ourselves through our illnesses
again and again
      day in dreariness
            night out of loneliness

Hoping for health
      hoping for the cure, the vaccine,
hoping that someday
the burden can be set down,
unpacked,
hoping that someday
we can pull out words
that shell iridescence around these old loyalties
we carry but cannot claim,
that someday we can pull out colors
from the trunk we've sheltered between us,
that trunk where colores y palabras keep coming and coming,
ready to wear in the world forever.

Conscientização

After Paulo Freire

They panhandled for pain,
traded beads of sweat for silver threads of theory
and rewove the golden rules into
rebozos to wrap the world in warm justice.
Over the years, the weavers multiplied,
the shawls materialized, or perhaps her eyes adjusted
to the darkness in the womb de la fuerza del pueblo.
She can see the material more clearly—
yards and yards of khadi, dyed into images by counting
finger-lengths of thread; fingers and cloth drenched in color—
images, distinct and intertwined, moving like lovers.

The dead and the newborn are laid in the cloth of the people.
The rest of us use it to carry our lives—
to hold close or to sling away.

They found themselves on opposite borders of a ripped rebozo,
the shawl slit, like young thieves slit screens to get back home,
like people become convicts— inadvertently at first,
then in anger and desperation,
frantic for any small change.

Entre Nous

There is a different way of speaking
which happens rarely and then only
between those who've loved so thoroughly
as to know a private shorthand
cut to the nucleus of not just what has been
but what is,
despite the deepest severance.

No Preference

Since you asked, no,
I would not choose women
before men,
or vice versa.
I can attract romance any style.
There used to be a fine-edged thrill
in attraction
but I tire quickly now
of these bouts;
can envision real passion
only in heightened friendship
of honest, equal people;
and find those true to me in life
ambivalent about my unorthodoxy.

Birthday in Maspeth

I.

Last June, I amtracked from heartland
to coast to desert to coast and back to the heartland.
A stranger plopped in beside me,
as we took off from Flagstaff at daybreak,
and for three hours
of Arizona countryside, we talked nonstop
as if, given only this space together,
we would condense our combined years
(a golden anniversary's worth of life)
into the glass bauble born of a morning.

II.

Blazing to a stop in Albuquerque with the late afternoon sun
I found a phone booth on the platform;
amongst newspapers, Indian artisans' silver,
burritos-with-green-chili, warm for the tracks,
I called up ten minutes of your voice,
          familiar, an oasis in our silence.
Afterward, the surrounding day draped heavily on my shoulders,
and I curled up on the blue seat to gain back lost sleep
as the hours were chiseled away on iron rails
          by an eastern trek into night.

III.

This year, the silence of your birthday diffuses into
my life on the east coast—
the school at the other end of that desert train trip called me
back for work on the island neighboring your home borough.
Here, I do not know where to put you,
amidst the superficial,
amidst the deeply untroubled . . .
our lines not broken, but untouchable, unvoiced.
Our silence, disembodied
as if my body itself were not present in my life here
where I pass only strangers
who do not plop in beside me to talk nonstop.

The agility of my affection keeps me in.
The agility of my angst keeps me out.
Are the words not spoken, if the line is dead?
Are words left off, unwritten,
when the PC goes off?
When no one on the outside craves my presence,
will I no longer materialize in the morning
with coffee and light?

Durga's Daughter

What if she bore a child
that was not her own
was no woman's
was only man's?

What if she bore a child like that?
Would that be more... more moral?
 If she'd dumped herself, afterward?
Would it have been a cleaner mess?

Maybe the sex of the fetus would have mattered—
male-encoded cells worth more than 35 years of female human life,
like in places where fetus gender is a matter of life or death,
like in places where human gender is a matter of life or death.

What if she bore a child
that was not to be her own
was no woman's
was only men's?

Would that be so unusual?
or more . . . more moral ?
Would that be so unusual in a place like here?

After the Unspeakable

"Will it be possible ever again to watch the slow,
amazed blink of a new-born gecko in the sun . . . ?"
— Arundhati Roy, October, 2001

Words pause among the geckos that hang about on stuccoed arches
framing my view of the yard's patterns and the road's rhythm.
In the white stucco I look for a trail off into the curve of logic
that must shape your deep silence.
I grasp for wisdom, settle for solace in Season.
The hummingbird, now absent, will visit my feeder again in April.
Hibiscus blooming alongside the marigolds this October will survive
the winter. Cold will come like a reptile's body in autumn,
followed, again by the warmth of mammals in spring earth's fleshy loam.
Your words as rare now as the breath of deep frost
in South Tejas Decembers may again leave footprints,
small kisses, besitos on the footpath. . . .
that will multiple with the strength of Mariposas Monarcas
      migrating south,
like blossoms on the crepe myrtle that shades a calavera calico cat.

Man is an Adjective

The thing is
that when she says
"he's a man"
that does not define
does not conscribe
it de-scribes:
wiggles the parameters
of the lines that guide,
bind, knot up
their attraction.

My lesbian friends would say
The thing to learn
if you are a woman
making sput with a man
making sperm with a man
making sense with a man
making it with a man,
is how to stop.

But if that doesn't work
I'd say the Big thing to remember
with a man
is that sometimes
he is an adjective
and either he knows it
and he's scared
or he don't even know
that he isn't always the subject.
and he ain't s'pose to be.
And I'm not talkin' adjectives like manly or macho
I'm talkin' manchild growin' up to be
man-friends
man-lovers
man-abusers

and I'm not talking man to man here
but woman to man; man to woman
woman to woman. . . .
I'm talkin' about you lovin' that man
who's making you out
as an adjective
and himself as the subject
all the time
and if you don't know it and do something about it
you're in for a bad case of penis worship
which hurts you cerebrum to aorta to vagina
and you don't know what hit you
because its as common and contagious as a cold
and you can get it from them or from us
and the only way to get yourself over it
and make yourself immune
is learning to catch it before it hits you
and you say' yup you're just an adjective,
Say, 'You may not be hurtin' me *because* you're a man
and I'm a woman—
cuz I've seen hurtin' happenin' in every combination there is
but you's hurtin' me this particular kinda way
because its a man-thing to do; a he-thing
and people will say—he's the man
he's gotta do it.
And he may say
she's a smart gal but she's a woman in love,
and I gotta tell her what's best . . .
And that's when you got to tell him
he ain't seein' right
'cause he's a man in love
and if he says he's not in love with you
remind him—that's not what you mean.
You've seen all the signs—he's a man in love with his self
and he better clear up that virus quick
'cause you don't wanna catch it;
'cause you may be a woman in love
but you got it under control by
knowin' it ain't that youz in love with a man,

and that if his being a man
is goin' to get in the way of youz bein' in love
you gonna try to get the Man part outta the way
and if that don't work you gonna get him outta the way
body and soul
'cause you like being in love
but you know that his being a man is just an adjective
like a flea on the cat of youralls' love
like a flea or like a ladybug sometimes—sorta cute, maybe good luck
and all, but if he's gonna think it means he's in charge
of anything about you or your love
then that's interference
and its time to call the play
over . . . You gotta write the next page.

Challenging Time Lines: On So-Called Fertility Votives

Was fertility
really the prayer
back then
when giving birth
was most dangerous,
when motherhood lasted from puberty
to old age?

I think women had other
things on their minds sometimes
while carving big clay breasts,
hollow eyes, massive hips

Maybe those women were
thinking of the emptiness
in the eyes of their 'special sons'
or the distinctive curve
of their women-friends'
warm, fat bodies,
or maybe they were praying for milk to swell
their breasts when the babies came again.

Maybe they were
contemplating what would be said
of their art in 5000 years.

Farewell Lines

Eulogy for Land Lines, Pay Phones, Pre-Cable & Pre-Converter Box TV, Telegrams, Reel to Reel, Video & Cassette Tapes, Kodachrome Film, Polaroids, & Even Eight Tracks

Life is less without you.

Ojos Verdes

I see your green eyes in my garden
in the new pea pods
and potato leaves,
in the canopy of pumpkin vine,
in the straight stalks of corn.
I see your green eyes
in the shadows of the oak
on my un-mown lawn.
The always changing green of your eyes
holds me close to the receding shadow
of your presence.

Chautauqua Finis

You drove out
toward Dakota
in your old Plymouth
big as a houseboat.
In this endless rain day,
it is fortunate
to be in a dry retreat
on an interstate toward summer
with a year's belongings
and a short wave.

I didn't see you leave
through dawn rain,
but said good-bye
at the Legal Tender last night,
exchanged odes in code-switch,
held you steady,
while your eyes darkened
to a shade I couldn't read for
we'd had time only for the dialect,
unfamiliar bodies speak.

Time Lines Curl Back

At the farewell party, old paper curling from recently denuded walls
of the old house drifts into our drinks.
The longhair lolls above us on top of a step ladder
that is more unsteady than anyone here;
the ladder jumps as we dance,
but the cat on top is motionless,
except for somber eyes
that move through us, moving.

Our eyes refract the shades of pleasure;
the cat's refract the red bulb that swings above dancing heads.
Desire is a deaf-mute now. We have become a married people.
There is nothing left to old rituals but good-byes.
On her hand, she wears the hard evidence well—she belongs.
She belongs to him, and to them, and I speak to him seldom
now, finicky with words,
lest one false start reveal the unspoken.

I step out on the porch with a cigarette and white fog curls into
the body of smoke, hiding the source of lunar light above.
Do those who know fog understand the similar density
that hangs between past tense lovers?—
our past, lost to grief that no one need touch anymore,
as if only the cat were sure enough to live again.

A party refines as it lengthens.
Excluded softly from the enclave of couples inside,
I belong to the fog . . .
until he comes onto the porch.
Paint curls. Fog curls. Gut curls.
"Leaving?" he asks. Time curls back upon itself.
The fog sets a scene for melodrama
on the house next door—moon emerges, full and white,
fills an empty white porch swing.
I say, "Did you know ?"

He says, "that it is the last full moon on Friday
the thirteenth until the year 2000."
"October." I say. "Thirteen years."
I move into the fog, and it catches me.

As lips close in

the distance between three oceans and three Halcyons implodes,
and as your tongue circles and dives,
the years' white noise drops away.
Fusion picks up an old jazz rhythm
in the slack of silence, and somewhere, as if phone lines are crossed,
someone hums a ballad, a corrido, with no narrative line.
For hours, I watch the contours of your face,
chalked blue in moon shadows.
I feel the firm warmth of your body as if
I would recognize it after a generation of Januaries,
by the familiar sense of its space against mine.

Dawn arrives without knocking
a heavy darkness lingers, a liquid stare that doesn't dissipate
even as you try to blink away the night, blink awake to day.
We grasp at the short silver hours
of winter light, not wanting to disturb time that even after implosion
continues the count in intervals. If only we had a say in Time's rule,
in the chasms that ripple from what is past, forward. But I,
great granddaughter of a Swiss watchmaker,
have no such sway with time.
We trudge out to part again on the edge of the ocean,
at the spot where, in half a dozen years a seam in time will be rent,
but without this precognition, we return to our respective islands
empty, absolved, and self-absorbed.

The awful white noise is gone, but the awkwardness of walking
across land strewn with a crumbled wall remains.
Indoors again, at last, I draw a blanket over the depression,
held in time, made by two bodies
in the sheeted mattress. I wonder if this is what is left
after an implosion—this emptiness. Your presence, distracted
by another loss, nonetheless comforted me,
and I could only return the favor.
What comes around, goes . . ., comes and goes

I don't know yet if I have comforted myself
or only felt your pain double in on me.
Only time knows,
only the wavering movement in the distance will reveal . . .
Not knowing what else to do as blue shadows return,
I light a candle—
continuity with the next light of dawn.

Mbuso's Farewell

The windfalls make a bitter sauce without honey
but that's how Grandma ate them;
so for June nights, unending June nights
I cut green apples
into small clean angles
boil them,
spiral them through the
Victoria Strainer
and pack them in freezer boxes
marked APPLESAUCE 1987.

That was the summer
he left to go
home to South Africa
with a degree in biology
and no chimera
but remembrance
of years passed together
and love cut short.

He'd tended his plants daily, sang to them,
kept pride in them. He gave them
to her when he left after graduation.
Four years of plants and his affection—
he left them all still growing
on the Kansas plains
knowing that his return
was contingent on global politics,
knowing that his plants
were safe, well tended, loved.

On Raymondville: a conversation

Autumn, 2007

"When she lost peace in the Detention Center
where tents were lit 24/7 like empty convenience stores,
the doctor gave her pills but my wife spit them out quietly.

Now she is back in her country
with her family; her four year old stayed here,
with her most trusted friend.
I visit the child, snap photos to send. On the phone
the girl is too shy to speak, but she giggles at her mother's voice. . . .

It happened when I had to make a Saturday business trip
and my wife came along to see the desert in bloom—
it was so beautiful in Spring.
They'd put up a new checkpoint, and by the time we saw it,
it was too late—border patrol had surrounded us. . . .
They let me bring some cloths to the jail the next day.

The attorneys here raise hopes
and take money.
ICE is kinder than the lawyers.
They'd let me visit in Detention—1/2 hour, sometime two.

My wife has a golden spirit though.
When she'd call from Detention,
she'd have someone behind her
and she'd tell me, "This friend doesn't have someone like you
to pay the call. Can you stay on line a little longer,
cover her call, too, so she can talk to her family?"

Nina's Poem

July 2000

Your spirit-image, still in brown and black and white
on the old city-dairy wall,
in the Barrio Jungle Mural where we painted you
with El Sol y La Luna, and the chuparrosas,
quetzal and white herons
at la cruz de los calles, San Jacinto y El Paso.
You engender respeto, Cat—no one has marked
on la gatita above the window.
Nina, you were not jungle cat, except in the mural
but a barrio cat, in the best sense, yes—familia.
A casa cat—your house was his . . .
La Reina, you made each casita your castle.
Even in Providence where snow and ice whitened everything,
you stepped gently, glided over the solid cold of the Northeast
offering solace, the warm flesh of el sol, your soul . . .

And when his Datsun truck's corazón was thrown
in the hills of West Virginia
and the monotone cold rain of the Northeast followed
us through two days of used-car-purchasing, book-shipping,
repacking, improvising a carrier—table turned top-down
on the roof of the new-old Toyota—
until we got homebound for Tejas again,
you became a lap cat, grumpy, but giving, taking comfort,
warming, being warmed, as we couldn't do for each other.

Nina, you were una gatita to be loved,
a barrio cat, in the best sense—familia . . .

In my furious hustle toward an Oregon summer,
before taking the long train ride
to the northwest tip of Occupied México—

I stopped for a visit and
your frail strength tugged at my heart.
At your command to halt, and chat, pet you,
I watched you burrow into the bag I carried—
you rubbed against the indigenous fiber of Peruvian burgundy weave,
as if the strength of the hands that wove that bag
and the sacred scent of fiber once living,
could rub salud off on you,
lengthen your life, like a curandera's limpia.
But when he told me I'd missed my goodbyes to you, Nina,
I knew we'd already said them that afternoon in early May.

For Grandma

(*RMG, 1900-1995*)

Beginnings and Endings meet in the lavender light
between Halcyon and January.
For you, Grandma, the road between beginning and end
was long, good and long. You chose to slip in and out
in these serene days—tranquil days in which the literature
of science and myth converge in the lore of life.
If humans have free will, as you, Grandma, would believe they do,
surely, then our first and last choices lie in when
to be born and when to die. Your choices,
like the life that connected them were gilded with grace.

It was at the solstices we saw you most.
We spent those days with you nearly every year—
Christmas time and summertime were long drives
toward that distant fat pedestal—
"Grandma and Grandpa's water-tower."
Your house meant color TV and chocolate, mints, corn candy
and walks around the tired, composed, remnants of a tiny town
in the midst of fields of corn and beans
where the seasons blend from brown to green,
disappear in whiteness, reemerge in dark sepia.

In winter, bundled cousins arrived from the warmth of the south
and we of the third generation slept beneath piles of blankets
tucked in under the silver tree downstairs, after, as the first or youngest
we'd each taken our turn at the cold upstairs trundle bed.
In summer, parentless vacations were spent with you—
endless days of novelties— color console, air conditioning,
gladiolas in the garden, the old wooden phone
        to ring Grandpa in his shop,
and in the evening, rounds of homemade ice cream—
we must have hit the socials of every denomination in Hiawatha.

You were always looking up the road,
guiding the growing-up of students, children, grandchildren;
you left your blessing
on our generation's first great grandchild.
How many crops of tomatoes and apples did you can, Grandma?
How many semesters did you teach youngsters
English, biology, goodwill?
How many of those big print condensed stories did you read
    in the Villa?
How many rides did you take with Grandpa
    in the big shiny Fords?
and you never learned to drive, so that in your old age,
you had to ask (so many times)
"when are you going to take me home?"
I guess you're getting home now
and Grandma, this time you *are* doing the driving.

Arriving on the eve of what would have been your 35th birthday

Kansas City is dull with gloom
even as we enter on dawn's bright arrival.
Dread caught up with me there
where they caught you fleeing your illness.
The city promised you rest, then turned on you
and in the dark emptiness
of a boarded up building
where no one could witness the screams
that pendulumed at odd angles
inside you, against you,
those boys thrashed into you
their pleasure: their base hatred bruising inside you
bruising right up into your heart
already so scarred that days later,
when you took life into your own hands
ended, once and for all,
the mutilation of your soul, brutalization of your flesh
the doctors could not pass on your heart
with the other organs, for the living.

Kansas City was only the last stop on the line for you,
the point where your vulnerability finally tipped
the scale against your immense strength.
After it happened, you did what should be done:
You walked to the bus station where you'd arrived
to escape the hospital only days earlier.
You called your sister, called the police,
led them to the building,
described the men, the rape.
You, who had not talked for months
finished your vow of silence,
summoned the strength to make an official report
of the crime that someone will always say we asked for.

But all the violence you'd held onto
these years, from those who've quit respect
imploded. You made the final cut
with the world that had given you such mixed messages.
The plastic that you hated
became your tool to wall off life's breath
till your own last whispers too
implode.

Lines for Manny

for Manuel Diosdada Castillo

I.

Could you paint birds
in a Barrio Jungle?
aves en la selva de este ciudad?
on the Westside, con San Anto?
With my "yes" to that question, I met Manny--

Manny, who deals in dreams, not dollars--
and asks for that
which makes tunes fly true,
asks for what is tucked close to corazón,
what few have ever asked of me--
like painting jungle birds on an old city-dairy wall,
things that make me say "I'd be honored. . . ."

II.

Buene Gente,
Take up the tools of mourning—
Pen, brush, roller and laptop
camera, guitar, drums and voice. . . .
Tears will not take a rain-check,
La luz del alma shines nonstop,
Our Barrio's corazón does not skip a beat,
as we honor her son, beloved,
with wails of color,
loud drums, rhythm, and paint.

Horizon Lines on the Prairie

Does the Paradigm of Language Overlap with the Paradigm of Prairie Sand Hills?

There is little
in the languages I've learned
to speak of little bluestem prairie
pastel brush strokes digitized by autumn
dabbed with yellow goldenrods
and the brown brackets of bundleweed
moving toward darkening oaks and flashes of sumac.

Within an October improvisation of Ohio evening
black, fat crows wing slow, raga rhythms across
a globe of sky—cielo de colores,
heaven hanging heavy with color.

May 23, 2:00 p.m.
Sand Prairie

"The primrose blooms here
only in May," she said,
motioning to yellow tones
and flesh petals, defying dead grass.
He strode forward
bent over
and pulled it up.

September 19, 8:15 a.m.
Walnut Valley

Cottonwoods stretch with morning wind.
Streaks of bird sound color otherwise empty air.
An airplane bomber cracks the smooth glaze
                                    of the blue bowl.

from Breeding Bird Census Poem Cycle, 1970s

June 27, 6:04 a.m.
Cottonwood Falls, KS

At sunrise
the wind turns,
stirs tallgrass
    that bends together and away
              together and apart . . .

White clapboard brightening with sun
rises perpendicular to flat green—
rectangles imposing on prairie golds.
       Grasses eddy against the wind . . .
          A cat steps out
crosses the dirt road,
pauses at a tin mailbox atop a darkened hedge post.
His ears pull up.
His long body dips sideways across the ditch.
He crosses the wet lawn
and settles on a dew-damp porch-step.

Ohio Prairie, 1986

I. Sunset—

Three weeks ago
barely the pause of blush
in the thicket.
This evening the sumac
and sandplum and creeper
the sun in her descent.

II. This barren sand, otherwise unmarked

A heron, a dog
a mole
and I have visited
since last night's rain.
Our marks, softened by wind
            Nothing else.

III. Oriole Cardinal Chickadee

Voices wrapped in wind.
Is it wind?
or is it cottonwoods' waxy June leaves
that hasten whirling minds to doze?

Vigilance

I watch the stones as I walk the dirt road
through the plowed field
but find nothing like the arrowhead
on the path by the creek.

On the Prairie

after too much time away:
I hear a patch of sand
whispering
and start toward it
looking out for buildings, trees
barriers
to go around,
but here my route is my own choosing.

Here Too Suspended

Perspective here is not flat but engulfing—
it holds me
like in an airplane suspended, still in atmosphere
of earth and I knowing that should the airplane be gone
I would fall back toward something I know
but have no choice in.
Here too suspended knowing
the other world where
teenagers make suicide pacts
and sit in cars like this one
like I am sitting, and die there
because of something that only
those who've seen could tell.
A pact is important at 15.
There is not much
you are willing to do alone.

Words on page never so soft-edged as these muted hills

Cottonwoods canopy the sand road:
a bare shore, smooth and the color
of my knuckles when my fist tightens on the steering wheel,
the width of two foreign cars
and the length of the Sand Hills spit up by the Arkansas
generations back.

We'd drive slow rolling out tracks
like the tracks of those who live here:
white- footed mice sandhill cranes white-tailed deer
hognose snakes; it was the snakes we wanted to catch.

It was this illusive peace, never lost,
post-human constancy that asks,
How can one marry but to some portion of the earth?
Twenty-five years is like a day here.
Only cars that pass me are different shapes than before.

Horizon Lines:
Returns to the South Land

Yatra en Norte América

Unaware, we are stragglers on the route
south from Aztlán—
on the foot-march scribed
by ancient scholars in records
burned away by imperialist visitors.
In México, people recognize
a past Austrian emperor in Renate's green gold eyes.
They look at my dark features with less interest.
If asked, I sometimes answer
"Yo soy Menonita, como el queso rico.

En Real de Catorce

I.

Take No Photo Here,
On the top of Leunar
the first of the earth
to be raised
by the Peyote God.
On the slab that Don Mescal bore,
people have placed small stones,
swathes of dark hair,
reeds, striped with paint and tied
with a woven strip of colors,
and dry flowers, wrapped with cloth.
Candles have blackened
the boulder, left their white waxen tears.
Coins, a corn husk
and a red chalked arrow align themselves
beside the slashes God made on granite.

Atop the rock,
pop bottle lids,
broken glass at my feet.

II.

Beyond the ruins
of the silver city
and before the slope
of Leunar, the holy mountain
where the God, Don Mescal gave
peyote to the world he'd borne,
we crawled over the cemetery wall
where twilight met the white shrine
of the old cathedral

and saw light moving toward us.
Renate said, "I think that UFOs
conduct business certain places
and certain places are more likely
than others. This place is
more likely than, for instance,
Bad Ischl, Austria, my home town
where the visitors are only tourists.

III.

Andrew's Birthday:

The Cathedral clock
chimes as the night turns,
and looking from the hotel roof
toward the neon cross in the sky
above the mountains shaded by half the earth,
I see Corona Borealis straight overhead
and remember. . . .

I lay wedged into a down mummy bag
with Alejandro the spelunker
no longer a stranger because
he spoke my language and laughed
at my jokes,
and wanted me there with a passion
like the women that afternoon in the cathedral
had wanted Mary and Jesus and the Saints.

I remember you in Ohio
where I hope the snows are over,
speaking of birthdays on the beach in Britain.
I hope you in zippered-on-sole tennis shoes, baggy shorts
straw hat receive some fragment of this
espiritu maravilloso tonight.

How I Studied Foreign Texts at Teotihuacan and Why I Stopped:

Obsidian trinket gods
machined arrowheads
plated steel jewelry
thrust in my face as I climb.
Rugs spread out up and down the pyramids
collect the smell of commercials in this desert.
At the top, racks of postcards
and a boom box "I don't need
you anymore." Mexican pop, English words.

A swallowtail butterfly
ripples from the top of the Aztec sun pyramid.

On the Caribbean

I. Reggae plays here

The bar tender in the thatched hut
napkin-wrapped the bottle
of dos equis that flashes in the wind and light—
a lullaby like angel wings
held intact on glass
by the sweat of compassion for the sun.

II. Tarde

Water Sky Wind Sand
darken with the afternoon
until moon makes light rise again.

IV. Night at Chetumel

Cloud-clothed, moon
splotches the ocean with shine.
Moon in the naked air:
ocean gulps
        the moon all over.

Over Lines in Sand

Cross Over the Line

The Mennonite in me, like the woman,
was taught the art of endurance,
of self sacrifice toward justice, pacifism or passion.
I'd die before ending a hunger strike made for the right cause.
But the time comes when hunger compels,
when the hunger of nonviolence drives
one to save oneself from death by neglect,
when hunger or thirst makes empty hands into bare hands
in order to free them, to tear out prejudice.

It is time to evoke another side of my ancestry—
to call forth the Deacon, Jireh, the English white man,
whose name I carry,
Jireh, a Congregationalist, whose gun over the threshold
marked a safety zone for Africans—
Americans on the freedom train.
Jireh who used white privilege
as a weapon against his neighbor's prejudice
to make a safe bed for a stranger passing through.
Those who would form the first klan
would come up to Jireh's fence,
with threats and horses.
but the Deacon and his wife were good hosts—
It is said, if need be he'd run out
brandishing insanity and his gun;
the men on horseback would back away . . . .
The most they left was a knife
embedded in Jireh's fencepost.

No one dared call it peace: 1993

Feeling relief that not too many body bag bundles came home
flesh, bones and blood of severed lives
does not mean tying yellow ribbons on buildings
like so many holiday packages
set out in rows across town—
the flesh, blood and bones
of hundreds of thousands was not bundled up
and swaddled in stars and stripes
but dumped in mass graves with no funeral processions
no flowers and no yellow ribbons.

La Despedida: Austin, Texas, 1992

Cristo Rey is white limestone rising
bright against the blue sky on a Tuesday morning.
From the street a dark line curves up the steps
into the spring green lawn
as young men clumsily shoulder
the weight of their loss—
brother comrade lover friend.
They wield a coffin draped with the colors of a nation
that turns a cold shoulder to the dark brilliance
and blinding needs of its youth.
The first people converge at the entrance;
followers wind like a slow snake dance across the lawn.
Black-haired heads gather together
making the surface of a rebozo gliding on wind
weaving its way into the opening of a wound—
the womb where a few springs back
the same dark heads emerged blessed with life and spirit.
In these times, the young must bury their lovers
before their grandparents.

Where were the Crows?

When Bhopal went
where were the crows?
Did they fly up from a roost
in the trees that would later
look like holocaust victims
in photos taken by foreign journalists?

Did they fly above the carbide-men-made gas?
Fly above and soar, like hawks
to watch, through a lens of transparent death
as mortals ran with the wind that held their final breaths.

Or did the gas take those crows like a witch:
"Crows flying in treetops...suddenly tumble,
swirling through the air dead."*

*The line and witch myth are from Mahasweta Devi's story
"The Witch-Hunt" translated by Kalpana Bardhan in *Of Women,
Outcastes, Peasants, and Rebels: A Selection of Bengali Short Stories*
(1990, 243). Ultimately it is revealed that the witch is an impaired
servant woman who has been turned out into the forest when she
became pregnant, the result of a rape by the master's son. The
witch threat story was started by the master.

brother, teacher, student, lover

Long Island NY, 1996
After "Sweet Honey in the Rock"

brother, teacher, student, lover
they can't keep you from my heart
but if we walk out together in the rain tonight
share this umbrella on this stormy night
walk from the fluorescent light
into the moon light
Will we walk from our hearts
into the barrel of a cop's gun?
into the crash of his lead pipe?
brother, teacher, student, lover
Black and white, Black and white
brother, teacher, student, lover

White Noise, NYC

Para las mujeres de Juárez

I.

I am walking down my street with my laundry
walking to my laundrymat, thinking about that white woman.
After the beating, men on the progressive radio talk shows
kept asking "where is that white woman?

Its hot even in my tank top and shorts; it's the first hot day of June.
To my right, a window slides open and shut again; curtains twist.
I am on the steps of the laundromat and a neighbor yells
in my direction
"hey, don't go in there.
They had a problem in there. Its closed."
I look at the door ajar, machines whirring, fans whirring.
I look back at him on a porch down the next block.
"OK" I say, "thanks."
I start back to my apartment at the other end of the block.

To my left, a window slides open. I look up.
A middle-aged white man is peering, leering at me.
I hear a sound from the window.
I turn away and walk fast.
I think about the white woman
beaten while jogging in Manhattan.
I think about the anonymous Latina
found dead in a ditch.
I think about the Brazilian jogger
murdered in Central Park.
I think about the Black woman
killed on the M train two stops from here.
I think about the un-described women
raped up the street in Forest Park and Ozone Park.
I think about the Chinese Filopina killed opening her laundromat.
I think about the Chinese Filopina killed in Upper Manhattan
at the door of her Laundromat.

I think of women who are bodies without killers.
I think of women who are without body and soul.

I am home; my apartment is locked behind me.
I've checked the closet.
I think about the white woman who was being walked to her car
when the student from my school put an iron pipe
to the head of her young Black friend
and the white man with the badge threatened bystanders
with a gun if they moved to help
if they were moved to help the Black man.
I think about that silent white woman.
I think about the white noise of the apartment around me.
We are living with the killers.
We are living with ourselves.

II.

I was going north that afternoon
that in de pendejo afternoon
that cuatro de Julio afternoon
north from la frontera de tierra de las reinas
y los reyes
north to the Bronx.
I was going north
when you were coming south
and our trains passed
in the night of the subway tunnel
I was that close to you then
but on the radio this evening
when I heard your mother wailing
I was that close to you again.

In that gun-powdered night I was going back south
when you were heading back north
north to Yonkers where you lived
with your family, told your dad good morning
everyday before his work

We were both heading back on the subway
and I passed near the station
that night
where he shot you in the back
where he shot you unarmed in the back
where he shot five times
shot you in the back.

I said good-bye to my brother in the Bronx
ran down and jumped
and I was inside, the doors closed
and the subway man laughed
at me, a white woman
who sure could run
who was lucky, he said.
And I laughed too cause I made that train.
that empty train.
We were way south of 167th street
before the crowd piled on.
The fireworks crowd going home
like you, like me
going home to sleep late
like your dad thought you were doing
when he went to work
and you didn't say good-bye.
I was that close to you
when your mother said,
"He always walked away."
when your mother said
"He always turned around."
when your aunt said
"We just want him back
and they still have his body."
The cops still have his body
they took his life
and they won't give his body back.

I was that close
but white, like the cop—not
but not Black like you
not a man, but a woman
on the subway that night
that in de pendejo night
that cuatro de Julio night.
I was that close
going back south
and you going back north
till they shot you in the back.
till they shot you in the back
and I got home and walked down
the block to watch my neighbors
flying Puerto Rican flags from their window
and shooting gunpowder and light
into that cuatro de Julio night.
because we didn't know then that you were already dead.

Seasonal Still Life, 2005

Strange fruit hangs once again in Texas.
"Francis, Francis, Francis*," the protestors chant.

Before their song dies, a million are fleeing the wind on the coast.

There is no homeland security to blanket this state where
bitter fruit swells with toxins riding in on the east wind.
Further east, buds burst after poisons sloshed about, and receded.
And I remember last winter's white blossoms of short-lived grace
after ice broke branch from trunk across the Kansas countryside,
after workers from Louisiana brought back the lights at
Meadowlark.

Egged on with environmental errors
made by an admin. with an attitude—
no global warning heeded here . . . no, sir—
Katrina killed a thousand, Rita threatens more . . .
and today, beneath the radar, beneath the fury, the State killed
Francis.
Her last words are muted by poison that grabs her tongue.
The words left their shape on her mouth afterward.

Strange fruit still hangs in Texas
"Francis, Francis, Francis." The wind chants.
Billie sings . . .

Strange fruit hangs again, again.

*Francis Newton was executed in Texas on September 14, 2005, one of ten
women executed in the U.S. in the decade following the 1976 death penalty
reinstatement; she had been denied a competent lawyer.

Esperanza, August 1998

When the smell of skunk
wafted in on the finally-rain-cooled breeze
and woke me, forcing me to close windows
and look for sandalwood left by an artist friend—
"a way to clear the mind" she says—
I searched my half packedforthemovedownFultonAve.
apartment thinking "its too bad almost no one
gives out matchbooks anymore."

When old match was found
struck on sandalwood
and glowing bravely in the funk
I thought of the Esperanza down on San Pedro Street
and how Esperanza's artetowardjusticia helps
clear the mind at 4 a.m.
I thought of a voice on the radio
yesterday morning saying
"we helped them hide from Nazis
so we would not lay awake at night."
I thought how hiding so often only equals death
and only the arte-es-vida survives hiding,
to help the rest of us find clear minds . . .

When sandalwood needed reinforcement
against stillseepingin skunk funk at 4:47 a.m.
(who says one needs no good house insulation in San Anto)
I lit Nuestra Lady candle
given by otra profesora de Incarnate Word last December
and began thinking about how the city defunding Esperanza
is sort of like forcing us artistas por justicia to go into hiding
and the Esperanza law suit announced yesterday
may do more than keep us awake at night
like the onda of ozone heat, rain y skunk—
like sandalwood and Guadalupe, it may help esta Ciudad,
may help us all clear our minds por la paz.

Las Manítas de La Paz

Halcyon days just passed through the Lacandon jungle
But that close to the equator days are always long, verdad?
Winter Solstice may have always meant something different
before the people rose up and called themselves Zapatistas,
before the people rose up and called for La Paz en la silva
                              justicia en el mundo.
Hands flew in all directions then
hands with weapons
            ripping prayers from the hands of women
tearing the petitions out of las manitas de los niños.

Hands flew in all directions then—
but USA y PRI were holding hands
dirty hands,
that killed forty five.
When those ninety hands went limp
the prayers they had cupped were given wings.

Hands flew in all directions then
and the hands of time
covered her face when she saw what was done
in that holiest of moments
as earth and sun turned back toward long caresses.
Time covered her face with her hands
when she saw what was done to the women
who were praying for peace.

Waterlines, 2005

Before Global Warming . . .

Summer ends with the fury of hurricanes
slamming open unnamed
depositories of toxic waste—
environmental enemas
cleaning out
what industry would not,
washing it onto Gulf Coast
homes and gardens.

In the flood waves
I hear ancient women
pound upon
this Pandora's jar
just as decades earlier
human protestors
pounded on trident
missiles to counter
radioactive militarism's rise.

No membrane, no levee, no condom,
no levee-wall,
Persian Gulf landing strip toxic
steel and concrete border wall
will hold back this water-borne release.
Abstinence will not protect us—
cover-up will not stop its lethal reach.
Even the dust to which we return is tainted.
In seven generations, perhaps, they will know what hit us.

Tonantzín

After media reports, 2-4-07

Guadalupe Tonantzin appears on the faces of tortillas
across the continent this week.

And los pueblos de México call out to her holiness,
call out against the doubling of prices for a kilo/day's worth of tortillas.

Call out against NAFTA & CAFTA,
the thieves that have colonized nuestra comida de la vida,
stolen ancient corn seed life
and sold Nuestra Señora's cape
to the lowest, sleaziest, neighboring bidder.

Los pueblos de México call out,
call out against the "little gentleman"
who follows the big blunderer whose wicked ways sicken the earth
as her inhabitants perish in the land
that cradled its cultura primera.

They call out against undocumented genetically-mutated Iowa corn
that has immigrated south on the wings of corp-profit.

Guadalupe Tonantzín appears on the faces of tortillas
in Chiapas and Oaxaca, in Guerrero and Michoacán, in Tamaulipas
and Nuevo Leon, in Coahuila and Chihuahua, in Aztlán.
Guadalupe Tonantzín's face appears on the faces of tortillas,
their cheeks brush and blush.

Nuestra Señora kisses the earth's brow
cools her fever, and warms the gente de maíz back to life.

Checkpoint

Traveling 281 north to San Antonio
outside Falfurrias and
we're pulled over to a checkpoint.
I hide my cat's eyes from the canines
that prowl and sniff at the vehicles.

The uniformed man
motions my window down
and asks "American Citizen?"
and with my Yankee-speak "yes"
and the dog's nonchalance about my pickup
La Migra ushers us past,
while others see their lives turned inside out,
forced into rendezvous with past places left behind.

Waiting in line, I had watched
while a vanload of immigrants were unloaded
and handcuffed. Glimpsing the face of one man,
I saw him cornered by despair.
I'd winced behind my car window
seeing something in his eyes—
at once too intimate,
and yet too public, to share with a stranger.

Checkpoints mark space with fear
like a tomcat's urine, sprayed,
drying putrid, but invisible.
I think of Israeli checkpoints
for Palestinians
and U.S. checkpoints for Iraqis
both, like here,
on occupied land.

I think of the hand-signals at Falfurrias
that I misunderstood, first time through,
the time the ICE-man yelled and my cat cowered
because I'd rolled forward when He meant for me to "stop—"
knowing at some checkpoints,
I might not live to remember false moves.
As I pull away from the checkpoint
my pickup stalls, the engine momentarily
stilled: the repose of the violence done here lingers.
My cat meows mournfully.
I pay silent respect to the earth beneath this spot
and all checkpoints tainted by the mean spirits of men.

In Support of the Troops Home Fast Against the War
written to a Lebanese friend

Meadowlark, July 2006

I.

I cannot fast
I eat halvah from Lebanon
("not to be nationalistic, but Lebanese halvah is the best"
you told me as we prepared Esperanza's feast.)

I protest the wars
balking against them with each breath of July-Kansas heat,
but I cannot fast against the heat of my country's aggression.
I drench my bread in Palestinian olive oil
to eat with heirloom tomatoes from my courtyard.
Despite your national loyalties you admit
Palestine makes the best olive oil—
pressed from trees that bore their first fruit
when your Christ walked amongst them.
I mix fresh mint from my father's garden
with dry mint from Egypt and serve my guests.

I eat from the vines and the stems and the branches—
abundant inside the circle of sycamore I built
when the wars began again.
Deeming my land sculpture a vigil against war,
I named the circle of storm-fells
"what comes around goes around"
because the sycamore bark reminded me of camouflage—
the clothing that hides the hearts of the young
so they can kill and be killed.
Inside the circle, I tilled and planted the prairie sod with
mints & manzanilla, chili & lemon balm,
frijoles verdes de Bangladesh & melon seeds from the west coast.

Apricots, rosemary, figs,
persimmon and pecan and pistachio—
I mix the flora of four continents
and make my communion with la paz
de Zapatistas, de Gandhi, de King, de Cesar y Dolores.

I cannot fast when the heat is on.
I eat to sustain strength & spirit . . .
I quench my thirst for justice and sanity
with sustenance of connecting with the peoples
my country and its coalitions and cohorts kill in my name,
but I startle at sudden sound-wind on the prairie
and semi on the bypass
as the nightwaves bring news of more bombs on south Lebanon
and emailed photos of the wars' maimed gallery my inbox.

II.

In the morning I find our peahen killed
by a Bushy tailed raccoon.
There is no blood, but the bird is mauled, her head is missing.
The war will not leave me
and the images of the night and the morning merge in my mind.
I hold onto connections, the circle that sustains . . .
but now, I can no longer eat.
I cannot fast.
I cannot breathe in the heat of the wars.

Soft Breathing

To a president who promised . . .

Sun-soaked, sounds warm February-chill in afternoon air
with comings and goings of a trillion cells, a million souls,
each one driving or sauntering toward something,
the sound of drilling into stone, metal clashing
bird calls and squealing brakes, a paleta vendor's bell,
and somewhere tucked inside this soundscape of the city,
the soft breathing of the family of a soldier
issued summons to a war
we've been told not to question . . . .
The soft breath of someone
who may be asked to drop a bomb we've all helped buy . . .
as we've come and gone, brakes squealing, metal scraping
as we've bought our paletas,
built our lives
done our service
done our time . . .

On the other side of earth from San Anto,
another world
touches
another soundscape
upon another
upon another
as sound travels
to the soft breathing
of a family listening
for the first bombings
of the new war
in the distance
and then, nearby.

Once upon a time

Para nuestras futuro

Once upon a time
there was the possibility
of pre-colonial paradise
where rich and poor
and light in hue and rich in hue
and men and women
and women and women
and men and men
and so on and so on
lived with lions and lambs
and everyone suckled each others' nipples
and no one devised capitalist schemes
to get all the milk
Once upon a time

Acknowledgments

In art gallery parlance, "on the line" speaks of an artwork hung on a level with the eye of the viewer. Those who have helped me put my words "on the line" in that sense, have not only helped me to sort out, consider, study, display, make beautiful and rant over experiences, visions, and struggles, they have honored me with their teachings. Foremost among my teachers have been my parents, but they do not come first—for I've drawn from the stories passed down from much earlier ancestors and hence my predecessors have entered my poetry.

I've learned from peers—tough friends, kind strangers, wise students—All My Relatives, Mitakuye Oyasin ... —to make the most of life personally and "planetarily" and here I have recorded those lessons. This book documents a few stray moments of learning, witness, and enchantment—and I am honored by all who've played a role: friends in these lines, those lurking nearby, or yet to appear. . . . These poems cover several decades, some came through memory, some through the immediacy of the moment—I have left them in their most honest state, though poetry making, like dreaming, has a way of sharpening and enlarging through the telling. *On the Line* is less autobiography or confession than a *testimonio* of times, places and people I've chosen to embrace with words.

Were it not that one afternoon on my way out of San Antonio to Eugene, Oregon, I chatted with Bryce Milligan at a Guadalupe Cultural Arts function about sending some poetry, I might never have put this collection together. I had sent a version of my MFA thesis out for publication, gotten discouraged at the lack of response, and was subsequently sidetracked by academic writing and publishing, progressive activism and the sense that somehow fostering others' learning and creativity was more important than sustaining my own. I owe a debt of gratitude for the taps on the shoulder along the way from Bryce and a few other colleagues, friends, family and students who gave me the reminders that my own work, too, was worthy; this collection is the result of that encouragement.

The artwork on the cover of *On the Line* is a torn paper collage by Carol Andreas, my family relative and my mentor and *compañera* in social justice, teaching, writing and art. When Carol's image of a woman balancing on / traversing the line, vine, rope bridge, came to mind, I knew it would fit the book's cover, exactly. My deep appreciation goes to Carol's sons, who have given permission for use of her art-piece, and to Bryce, who used my idea for cover art, and honored it perfectly in his cover design.

Previously published poems include: "Tonantzin," in *BorderSenses* (Spring 2007); "Seasonal Still Life, 2005" in *BorderSenses* (Spring 2006); "My Own Private Borderlands" in *BorderSenses* (2003); "Esperanza, August 1998" in *La Voz* (1998); "Hibiscus and Marigolds" in *Catfish Poets Society Collection* (1992); and "Soft Breathing" in *Poets Against War*, online collection, www.poetsagainstthewar.org.

About the Author

Dr. Kamala Platt's first decade was shaped by family legacies in human rights work and life on the prairie in rural Kansas. She began writing as she learned to read, and her mother, herself a writer, encouraged her daughter's interest through a summer class with octogenarian poet Cora M. Nicodemus. Subsequently, Platt took poetry workshops with (listed chronologically) Beinvenido N. Santos, Victor Contoski, Keith Ratzlaff, Raylene Hinz-Penner, Howard McCord and Al Young.

Kamala's first trip across national borders was to the wedding of her uncle and aunt in Chihuahua, México, and in 1970, her family returned to Orissa, India where her parents had married in the late 1950s. There, Kamala met the woman after whom she is named, and others who were part of the AFSC Barpali Village Service Project's extended community. Mennonite voluntary service camps afforded her continued trans-cultural growth when her family returned to the U.S.; her first "official" teaching was in a Cheyenne Arapahoe summer school and her first sunrise walk after a night of conversation she experienced at Koinonia Farms.

During college, Kamala enrolled for a semester at the Urban Life Center on Chicago's southside. In Chicago, she began working with public art projects, in particular, murals, helped with the founding of The Peace Museum, and taught in the Westside's Public Arts Workshop. These experiences honed her sense of art as a force for social change. After graduation from Bethel College, where Kamala earned degrees in art, international development and religion, she returned to Chicago to enter an Interdisciplinary Arts Education graduate program at Columbia College where she became involved in performance art, using her poetry in conjunction with visual art, movement and sound; she also worked on the prep crew at the Museum of Contemporary Art, taught weaving courses at Gads Hill Community Center in Pilsen and Painting Poems for young students at the Chicago Public Library's

Cultural Center. Subsequently, she spent time in Lawrence, Kansas at University of Kansas (her parents' meeting place decades earlier), where she studied fiber, performance art, creative writing, and other coursework that contributed to her interdisciplinary work. During time away from schools, she managed her grandparents' house in North Newton, Kansas, and tried making a living as full-time artist. Her decision to seek an MFA in Creative Writing led her to Bowling Green State University (BGSU) in Ohio; there she worked toward self-definition as a writer in a world torn apart by war and injustice.

Completing her MFA in poetry, and interested in the theory that adhered art to life, Kamala moved to Austin, Texas, for a PhD in Comparative Literature from the University of Texas; in addition to her coursework, Kamala learned much from Austin's south and eastside communities: the Catfish Poet's Society, PODER, and Raúl R. Salinas' Resistencia Bookstore where in 1997 she defended her dissertation.

Much of the past two decades Dr. Platt spent in south Texas studying and/or teaching in academic departments—English, Bi-Cultural Bilingual Studies, Women's Studies.... Besides Westside, San Antonio, where Kamala has established a permanent residence, she lived in New York City for two years, while teaching at Nassau Community College; in Eugene, Oregon, while researching women's environmental justice cultural poetics through University of Oregon's Center for the Study of Women in Society; in Albuquerque's South Valley, while at University of New Mexico, where she received support for further environmental justice research; and in the Rio Grande Valley, where she currently teaches at the University of Texas–Pan American.

She has also, for the last half decade, directed the Meadowlark Center in Kansas, located on a rural acreage where Kamala's grandmother had built Meadowlark Homestead in the 1950s The Meadowlark Center hosts community arts, education, environment and social justice projects and events, and is revitalizing original passive solar design buildings, and restoring prairie and riparian habitat in line with the land's natural history. It offers alternative programming, meeting and exhibit space for both surrounding communities and eco-justice communities more broadly.

On The Line was born of Kamala's master's thesis at Bowling Green State University. Bryce Milligan of Wings Press asked her for "some poetry" in 2000. That original thesis, after ten years of revision, evolved into the present volume.

Wings Press was founded in 1975 by Joanie Whitebird and Joseph Lomax, both deceased, as "an informal association of artists and cultural mythologists dedicated to the preservation of the literature of the nation of Texas." Publisher, editor and designer since 1995, Bryce Milligan is honored to carry on and expand that mission to include the finest in American writing—meaning all of the Americas—without commercial considerations clouding the choice to publish or not to publish.

Wings Press publishes multicultural books, chapbooks, CDs and DVDs that, we hope, enlighten the human spirit and enliven the mind. Every person ever associated with Wings has been or is a writer, and we know well that writing is a transformational art form capable of changing the world, primarily by allowing us to glimpse something of each other's souls. Good writing is innovative, insightful, and interesting. But most of all it is honest.

Likewise, Wings Press is committed to treating the planet itself as a partner. Thus the press uses as much recycled material as possible, from the paper on which the books are printed to the boxes in which they are shipped. All inks and papers used meet or exceed United States health and safety requirements.

As Robert Dana wrote in *Against the Grain,* "Small press publishing is personal publishing. In essence, it's a matter of personal vision, personal taste and courage, and personal friendships." Welcome to the Wings Press community of readers.

Colophon

This first edition of *On the Line*, by Kamala
Platt, has been printed on 55 pound Edwards
Brothers Natural Paper containing a high per-
centage of recycled fiber. Titles have been set
in Papyrus type, the text in Adobe Caslon type.
All Wings Press books are designed and pro-
duced by Bryce Milligan.

On-line catalogue and ordering:
www.wingspress.com

Wings Press titles are distributed
to the trade by the
Independent Publishers Group
www.ipgbook.com
and in Europe by
www.gazellebookservices.co.uk